Short Days,
Long Shadows

Sheenagh Pugh

Seren is the book imprint of
Poetry Wales Press Ltd.
57 Nolton Street, Bridgend, Wales, CF31 3AE
www.serenbooks.com
facebook.com/SerenBooks
Twitter:@SerenBooks

ISBN: 978-1-78172-156-8
e-book: 978-1-78172-157-5
Kindle: 978-1-78172-158-2

A CIP record for this title is available from the British Library.

The publisher acknowledges the financial assistance of the Welsh Books Council.

Author's website: http://sheenagh.webs.com/

Cover photograph by Michael Burns

Printed in Bembo by Bell & Bain Ltd, Glasgow

Contents

Extremophile

Two miles below the light, bacteria
live without sun, thrive on sulphur
in a cave of radioactive rock,
and, blind in the night of the ocean floor,
molluscs that feed only on wood
wait for wrecks. White tubeworms heap
in snowdrifts around hydrothermal vents,
at home in scalding heat. Lichens encroach
on Antarctic valleys where no rain
ever fell. There is nowhere
life cannot take hold, nowhere so salt,
so cold, so acid, but some chancer
will be there, flourishing on bare stone,
getting by, gleaning a sparse living
from marine snow, scavenging
light from translucent quartz, as if
lack and hardship could do nothing
but quicken it, this urge
to cling on in the cracks
of the world, or as if this world
itself, so various, so not to be spared
as it is, were the impetus
never to leave it.

Come and Go

He has chosen, far nearer the end
than the beginning, to live
where, every day, he can watch the land

come and go, each time gleaming as if
it were new made. Sandbars shoulder
into the sun, their whereabouts too brief

to map, never drying out. Under
its pulsing skin the sea echoes
sunlight, shadows the clouds, goes undercover

in mist. What it is to be bodiless,
boneless, to reshape, to fill
with yourself the moulds of coves and bays,

take yourself back. He walks mile
after mile, blanking aches, stays up late
in the blue half-light, resists the pull

of sleep while he can, while his sight
still serves him, before that jerry-build,
his body, can no longer house a spirit
still nowhere near done with the world.

Staying

The ground beneath our feet
is shifting, has been on the move

for ever. This fissured sea-cliff
travelled north from the equator;

its heights were once an ocean floor.
Ice carves out rock, forests harden

to diamond as the stars burn down:
there is nothing that is not on a journey,

no abode for those who long only
to stay. We could be at ease

with so little, if it were for always:
a moment, a loved place. How modest

this aim to go nowhere, this least
of wishes, not to change our state.

Walker

1.

He is coming from the shore meadow
where oystercatchers landed today;

they are pairing, nesting, and he
moves like the shadow of a gull

across the grass, over a grey wall
laced with green, honeysuckle buds

gleaming. He steps between the blades
of daffodils. The woman never sees,

firming plants in her garden, as he passes
her by, slips in at the door open

to let sun and air in on her man,
getting some rest, seeing his flowers unfold,

watching the resurrection of the world
while he waits for his next bout of chemo.

2. His Colours

He sports the jester's coat,
red and yellow;

he is all in a glow
of falling leaves, bonfires

that throw out splinters
of light. His feet crush

berries into a blood-splash
on the paving-stones.

His colours: slanting suns,
clouds briefly ablaze,

he comes as a surprise,
this flaunting dandy

whom we had looked to see
in a plain black suit.

3. Gardening

White stones shaped like hearts:
you can tell they were chosen.

In the winter garden
they gleam on bare ground.

Hooded crows land
on the hard seed-beds,

frost crazes the buds
of a leafless rose.

The gardener, indoors, has eyes
only for the woman resting

more and more, who will not see spring
undammed in a blue rush.

Forget-me-nots lie in ambush:
the stones are shaped like hearts.

4. Him Again

He moves the way light moves: now sudden,
racing up a field as sun clears cloud,

now unnoticed, leaching from the world
until you look up into dark.

And he inhabits next door's peat stack,
waiting for winter, and the fat sheep

ready for the show, and the gap
in the window of what was a house

and is a shed, and soon will be out of use.
The berries that were once white blossom

on the brambles belong to him,
so they say, and lose all their taste

on a certain day, when he comes to harvest
what is alive, and ripe, and his own.

5. The Edges

He hangs around the edges
where things happen,

the shoreline where land is eaten
and shells wash up

empty. Where countries stop
midstream, or at barbed wire

and rifle posts. Where walls meet air
at windowsills, balconies, parapets.

Most often, though, he waits
on time's borders, the rim

where light and dark bleed, become
other, the red pen-stroke

that is Walker, his mark,
the end of days.

Days of November 2009

Short days, long shadows:
sun rising low skims the hill.

Mending, making good, days full
of outdoor jobs, folk

racing to finish before dark,
before winter. Angled light, always

on the edge of leaving. These days
when every little thing feels urgent,

unmissable, when all you want
is to hold on to a lit rack

of cirrus, the taste of woodsmoke
catching your throat, a sleek seal

slipping back under, the farewell
of geese, scribbled in black arrows.

Walsingham's Men

1. Player-Man

Maliverny Catlyn, "11", 1586

He writes this time from the Marshalsea,
having contrived to be confined
with two priests enchanted by a man
so willing to listen. He signs himself
"11". There is news to impart
only for the ears of his master,
touching insurrection.
                                    The spymaster
frowns slightly. He knows he must see
the fellow. 11 is a find,
one of his best, but a disturbing man
somehow, so *intense*. He himself
is reckoned puritan, yet for his part
he does not bar pleasure, apart
from the vicious sort. A Christian should be master
of his passions.
                        "Pray send them over sea,"
writes 11, "or let them be fined
or hanged, but prison them not, for one man
in prison draws many to himself
and his cause: prison is itself
their nursery."
                        Time this agent should depart
for the north, reflects the spymaster.
The recusant nobility will see
one of their own; 11 is refined
in manner, can act the gentleman
to admiration. Or any other man:
the wonder is, he still has a self
left to know. What is he, apart
from others, in his heart? Master
of appearance, he makes men see
what he says is there. He is defined

by otherness, like a mask you'd find
and try on.
                    Yet this is the man
who wants theatre banned, torments himself
to think how the full benches play a part
in emptying pews. He harangues his master
whenever they meet: *can you not see*
the evil in a man no one can find,
forever acting a part?
                              The spymaster
smiles: what he can see, he keeps to himself.

2. The Royal Purveyor of Poultry

Nicholas Berden, alias Thomas Rogers, 1588

Today he managed to get out
of the office for once. No holiday,
just inspecting some chickens in a garden,
a new source of supply.
                          They looked good,
fat and white. He bargained the price
thriftily down, as became his trust,
noting how they gathered, full of trust,
round the woman shaking scraps out
of her apron.
                  He needs thirty a day
for the court. But he counts it no burden:
he is a man who sees only the good
in his place. Assessing geese, putting a price
on chickens. Some dullness is the price
of safety. He tends to mistrust
new suppliers, always cautious, but out
in the air, heavy with lavender, today
he loosened up, chatted. Nothing hidden
in her face; she over-valued the goods,
but that's normal.

Everyone thinks their god
the best, their chickens beyond price;
he should know. Why else did they trust
him so, those careless priests he caught out
whispering and conspiring, in the days
when he wrote in cipher, when silence was golden
and no name but his own was forbidden?

They never saw beyond what seemed good
to them; could not suppose he might prize
some other good. Of course, you couldn't trust
their oath: all that loyalty they poured out
on the scaffold, when just the other day
he'd had them looking forward to the day
they'd turn the state upside down. A den
of snakes.
        Well, their war came to no good,
and with peace sure, he claimed the price
of service: a life in the open. And his trust
was not misplaced. The secret's out

for a burnt-out agent, Master Berden,
the best in his day, now happy to price
poultry. A place of trust. Life is good.

3. Decoder

Thomas Phelippes, alias John Morice,
alias Peter Halins, 1598

When, in the street, he catches foreign words
– Spanish, Italian, French – he can sense
his thought shifting, see the world remade,
but if the language be one he does not know,
he follows, caught, longing for sounds to resolve
into a pattern, to begin to *mean*
something.

This maggot has been the means
of his advance; it is not only words
he has a feel for. He can make sense
of symbols, letters, language unmade
by cipher, a crafted chaos he knows
for a world, for plans that dissolve
in the code's chrysalis, and will resolve
again to damn their authors. All means
of ciphering can be unlocked: the words
run together, the strings of nonsense
that mask how sentences are made,
the nulls, the substitutes.
                                   He seeks to know
what the enemy knows, what they think he knows,
to read their mind's language, to solve
their uncertainties, decode what they mean
to do. When sometimes they put into words
less than he knows they think, he turns the sense
to speak the truth. Their letters remade,
he sends them on their way, having first made
copies for all who need to know.
Some trust to alum ink, that dissolves
and fades on the page; he reads it by means
of fire. Their cipher keys, their passwords
open to him. People see him, and sense
no danger: so small and thin, in no sense
memorable, a null.
                          His fortune's made,
yet, for all the languages he knows,
figures are the code he can't solve,
the closed book. His debts many, his living mean,
he will get out of jail only with words,
demeaning himself to men who see sense
in his accounts, that wordless hash, who know
how to solve his life, the mess he's made.

Terra Nova

Cardiff Bay: 23rd May 2008

We'd taken him there for his birthday
– his last, as things turned out.
The Bay was new territory

to him ("getting the bus these days
feels like an expedition")
but he took to the place,

sipping red wine, chewing steak
slowly and thoughtfully, watching
swans, yachts, the crazy wake

of the ribs zipping to and fro
in the pleasure-lake that once
was a coal port. Sun at the window

ironed out his face. The hazy barrage
pleased him, and the herons,
and the sailors' church,

though he couldn't walk as far
as the man of ice,
the white mosaic sculpture

that marks the fool's errand
of a ship leaving safe harbour
to seek the world's end.

Travelling with Ashes

On the outskirts of town, we passed a dead factory,
windows all gone and the light pouring through,
airy and bright, a red-brick filigree.

At a disused halt, the edge of the platform
had blurred back to grass, and willowherb grew
through gaps in the flags and the crumbling asphalt.

And crossing the bridge, the stretches of mudflat
shone like lead sheets as the tide withdrew,
not looking as if it were planning a comeback

to float the bleached boat, an empty ribcage,
bones standing out as old men's do
when appetite's gone and flesh is wreckage.

Rust in the scrapyard was engraving
on heaps of silver and black and blue
some cryptic message to do with leaving,

and sunlight's morse sent answering flashes
off broken windscreens, a code he once knew.
Ciphers read clear, when you travel with ashes.

Medals

1. Pacific Star (India)

He used to swear a fog of spices
came curling over the sea
to grip his throat, a day out of Bombay.

Ashore, he broke all the rules, ate fruit
unwashed, pastries from street stalls,
drank the water, took no harm, loved it all.

One day, reading email from Rajasthan,
where his granddaughter is on her travels,
he will smile almost like a young man.

2. Africa Star (Egypt)

Egypt and he got off on the wrong foot.
Cairo, Alexandria, names of romance
merely curled his lip.

Young as he was, wide-eyed, he saw only
squalor and thievery. Never a good word
nor a fond memory.

Not the land's fault. How could it know
the glum sailor scuffing a stone
along the quay,

so far from home, was wishing himself
happy birthday, turning twenty-one
without ceremony?

3. Atlantic Star (Norway)

The best part of a day to sail
that long, branching fjord,
and we hardly left

the ship's rail. Molten-silver
waterfalls, the clash of white
where ice met cloud,

sentinel firs
loaded with snow, sea-eagles
skirmishing ahead.

Round every bend
something unmissable. He turned
the photographs, nodding.

"We sailed up there, looking
for the *Tirpitz*, hoping
we wouldn't find her."

4. Russian Convoys (North Cape)

Mid-afternoon
      no daylight left,

the Arctic Ocean
      a monotone

far below
      the edge of Europe.

Warm rooms cut
        deep in the rock,

café, souvenir shop
        and a plaque burnished

for all the young men
        sick as dogs

who could not come in
        out of the storm.

"Hell of a place
        to spend Christmas"

– though, he'd always add,
        worse for the prey,

the shapely *Scharnhorst*,
        her radar blinded,

pack closing in
        and no way home.

Uniform

Blue jeans, baseball cap, leather jacket,
white hair, why not? He's kept the uniform

of what he used to be: he won't become
his father, won't assume the cardigan.

And permanent waves are ebbing: the women
whose mothers resigned themselves at sixty

to ice-blue curls have stayed with bob and blow-dry.
These days, you're as old as you feel,

that's what they say, and age will not steal
the time of their lives: they will keep the dress

and music of their youth when they pass
through the curtains, which will close together

as neatly as they did to *Cwm Rhondda*
behind my father in his good suit.

Wedding Night in the Snow Hotel

Maybe she was playing at Kay and Gerda
– there was even a reindeer, wandering

through the fairytale; she stroked its stiff fur
and felt she had become fiction.

Inside the white walls, ice sculptures
drank light and altered it. She breathed

air that somehow seemed to lie
above the cold, distilled.

At the ceremony her words and his,
leaving their mouths, formed small nebulae

in the shapes of "take" and "give",
speech-bubbles bursting. Later, they sipped

cloudberry vodka from ice glasses
that somehow failed to burn their lips.

Maybe it was something about extremes
and contraries, huddled in their sleeping bag,

knowing they would never feel warmer
than on a bed of ice. The shared

lack of comfort, the laughter
next morning as they scrambled into clothes

on the snow floor, made a dash for the stove
in the kitchen hut next door.

Maybe. But when she scrolls through
the slideshow, what pleases her most

is knowing those photographs all show
rooms, corridors, bars, sofas

that aren't there any more, that melted
with summer, that will be rebuilt

with different snow, as a tale
differs for each listener.

What He Saw, Vesterålen

Out on the ice, he huddled by his lamp
on an upturned bucket, watching
the hole he'd drilled, dreaming of the gear
to be found online, heated ice shanties,
gas augers, sonar. Nothing was biting.
By and by, on the far side of the fjord,
lights came on in houses.

About then, he says, he began
to think the dark no longer empty,
to hear breathing in it. He felt observed.
His wife is a churchgoer; she would say
we are always observed, but he believes
what he sees. Still no tug on the line;
he thought about switching to emerald shiners
and sensed a silent concurrence all around,
the air nodding. Ice prickled in the breeze,
stung his face. A rosy bruise
spread in the east; he wondered if,
when the dark lifted, slabs of it might stay,
troll-like, petrified by light.

          He fixed his gaze
on the hole, its edges hardening
as his lamp faded. Shadows
formed on the ice; he looked up
and saw them, a ring of sea-eagles
waiting in patient reproach for the guts
of his uncaught fish. They hunched forward,
barbarian kings in shaggy black trousers
under great cloaks of bronze, gold-edged feathers
lapped like scale armour. They were so close,
he could see their blank amber eyes.

He counted thirteen, when he could count
at all. He told this at work, distracted,
pausing often to find words, mistaking
the change.

Pomor

ca 1700-1917

The people-by-the-sea
live at the world's roof,

trade across ice and ocean
and customs posts that exist

mainly in the minds of officials
a long way south.

Their fish and flour
outlawed, till the law gives in,

– as well tax gulls – they ignore
all borders on all maps,

Vardø and Arkhangelsk
their twin capitals, Russonorsk

their language of traded words.
Ideas are bartered

as freely as goods,
revolution stashed

in a sailor's pocket,
a bale of furs. One day

Lenin will do what kings
could not; seal off

the world's most permeable frontier.
Salmon, hemp, silver fox

and two alphabets
will stay their own side,

Finnmark will forget
how to count in kopeks,

as they did in the days
when a traveller wrote

it is as if men could live
without borders, taxes or princes.

Trondheim: January

You try to get a handle on this town
and it comes back to the hooded crows

foraging in snow, as everyday as sparrows,
but civil: no brawls. Grey-robed, black-capped, they wait

by the Justice Museum where the hangman's receipt
lists prices; so many kroner to take off

a hand, a head. They venture a throaty laugh
at the children sledging downhill

from the fort, do sentry-go outside its wall,
where the resistance men lay in their blood.

By the frozen river they promenade,
their suits shabby-genteel against the white:

elderly flâneurs in the strange pink daylight,
trading reminiscences, now and then.

Fogbound

Mist came walking in from the sea
over the island; it fingered

the very windows; outside
was nowhere to be seen.

There glowed, now and then
through the white, the yellow nimbus

of headlamps, and past the ness
drifted the muffled sound

of ships' foghorns. Behind
all this, though at the time

it was hard to credit them,
lay roads, houses, sunlight,

mail planes at the airport,
no end of blue sky.

Big Sky

Unbroken by forest or town, this skyline
all hills and ocean: you look up
and your gaze, stopped by no branch, no office block,
overflows with sky, too much to take in
even when you turn slowly in the circle
of green and blue. Who knew how vast
cumulus could boil over, or how sweeping
the great ragged brush-strokes of cirrus,
or, at night, how many bright worlds,
hundreds of years away, cluster and prickle
above our heads? It is as if,
having lived all your life in the jewelled oval
of a miniature, you stepped into a frame
the size of a gallery wall, a landscape
where a few small figures, lost against distance,
seem to be looking for the way out.

Living in a Snow Globe

Not so much a white-out
as a white-in, a dense swirl,

flinders idling, spinning out the fall,
filling the eye's field, muffling

all sound beyond a circle shrinking
to the point where you stand, slowly

turning, thinking you might be
living in a snow globe, a glass

curve that distorts and distances
the outside, the small silenced township,

while, this side of the wall, a whole landscape
turns upside down around one figure

fixed in a shaking flux and unsure
where here is, or how to get out.

Gannet

holds still in air, focuses far below,
then falls, dead straight, on the glittering fishdot
that rushes up to meet him.

His eye so keen, the sea
to him a pane of clear glass
that shatters to a dazzle

as he nuts it. He's a heid-the-ball,
lives in the violent moment, pure joy,
even the pain exploding

with each head-butt. Never thinks as far
as the floaters swimming
into his eyes' field,

the thin filaments fingering
their way across the iris,
the webs of blood

that will blur, one day,
into a blindfold. When he can't see
to dive, he will find a rock

and starve, unmoving, feel
sun and air pass him by, remember
the fall through light.

Sea's Answer

I was talking to the sea the other day,
(you get that way, at my age)
and I said, I wish I knew why,

when I figure you, every image
fails me. They are, after all, accurate,
for what that's worth: the scalloped edge

of lace, the beaten metal sheet,
pewter under cloud, copper at sunrise,
the pleated silk, anyone can see it,

and if they have been seen by many eyes,
still they are none the less true
the thousandth time. I don't believe in clichés;

words don't just stop working. But you
swallow each likeness, each true word
and spit it out, rejected; how

does *that* work?
                            Its stony throat wide,
the sea yawned, breathed out with the hawk
of a consumptive, and answered

"I am not *like* anything; you speak
of things made or named in my honour,
out of your own hunger, to be like
me. I am myself the metaphor."

Dresden Shepherdesses of 1908

They pose in their carnival costume,
gazing patiently into the lens,
waiting to be fixed for all time

as a group of china figurines.
The four in front, seated, arrange crossways
their dainty crooks, twisted with ribbons,

whose lattice pattern mirrors the laces
on their bodice fronts, below the frills
of the spilling collars, below the faces

crowned with roses, framed in tumbling curls,
the heavy features that don't pretend,
for a moment, to be other than male.

It's plain too in the way they stand,
the six at the back, grounding their crooks
like rifles. Tight-laced, white-gowned,

they plant their boots foursquare and black
beneath flounced skirts. Mothers and wives
have been busy with a pattern book,

letting out waists, lengthening hems and sleeves
to make them look perfect; you can see
the pride they take. Stepping out of their lives

for one night, the night they can be
who they like, alter themselves to fit
whatever otherness takes their fancy,

clerks and boatmen assume the exquisite
frivolity of ornaments, the dress
of a past time, choosing to inhabit,
for this one night, their inner shepherdess.

Blue

In the high window, looking out over
Hoswick Bay, a little blue boat
that sails nowhere, her light canvas
spread to the breeze that never blows
on the airless landing. Set on some pond,
she would float, I think, in fair weather,
given the chance, but she was not made
for the open sea, this painted toy
between the curtains, forever safe
from winds and waves. She has the lines
of a lady, though, as sailors say,
a craft that would answer. Sometimes a walker,
passing the house, will glance up
and pause: you can see his eyes fill
with the blueness of her, the promise
of movement, the framed story.

The *Viceroy of India*

When he was young, he says, this sound was choked
with shipping. He'll tell you, if you listen,

how, as a boy, he'd see his dream sail in,
the *Viceroy of India*, cruise vessel

among workboats, her famed swimming-pool
promising paradise. Then they took her

for a troopship, and him for a sailor;
he was on the *Boadicea*, off Oran,

when he saw her rakish lines again
and smiled, his mood lifting, a scant heartbeat

before the torpedo ripped her apart.
He helped pick up survivors, thinking

of the pool, and home, and yet another thing
that wouldn't be the same when he got back.

Tea with Skuas

Sailing close under a raucous bird-cliff,
craning their necks, the passengers choked
on the ammonia reek, unlooked-for but logical,

if you think about it. After a while
they scarcely noticed the glossy curious heads
of seals observing them from a distance.

When the first gannet fell, dead straight,
glinting into the waves after fish,
most of them, open-mouthed, missed it on camera,

but they soon got the hang of watching
only through the lens. They were getting blasé
by the time the captain found calm water,

killed his engine, assembled a trayful
of china mugs, asked about sugar
and poured tea, carefully, as you do

at three o'clock out on the North Sea.
Biscuits were handed round, there was small talk
and the captain, leaning over the rail,

arm at full stretch, held a digestive out
between thumb and fingertip. Eyes widened
as the great skua balanced overhead;

they'd all feared them out on the moorland
buzzing intruders, skimming the hair
of the unwary. They had not thought

to meet those claws, those cold eyes
so near. When it swooped, they ducked,
shielding their faces, squinting up to find

an empty hand, all fingers still present
but no biscuit. The predator following, screaming
for more handouts. The laughter, incredulous,

relieved. Next time it came down low
to seize its prize, they kept their heads,
captured it on film, between sips and nibbles.

The Madonna of the Rocks

She was in a narrow crevice
on Eshaness; she looked up
as they looked down

into a small, savage, pure white face
to take the breath away.
Lifting her lip

over tiny ivory knives, keeping
her kits behind her, she stood
her ground, staring

defiance at the giant faces
who could not tell her
they too were parents,

could only admire how she spat
come on if you think you're hard enough
at Herod's army.

Hecklers

Herring gulls are screaming slogans:
à la lanterne, whadda we want, out, out,
taunting. *Nobody likes us, we don't care.*
Their anarchic joy is catching: the way
they snatch what they fancy, the front
of their begging: *I want, you got, gimme.*
They know no shame, no betters, no place,
plebs at their ease; what does it matter
who thinks he's a bigwig, a VIP,
when they can bomb his bespoke suit
from a height, skim his hair, drown
his prepared soundbites: *you're not the boss of me!*

Three Poems from Unst at Midsummer

1. Treasure Island

No profit in buttercups, more's the pity,
or many a field on Unst
would yield a fortune.

2. Spendthrift

Fionn must have passed this way,
that profligate man
with a hole in his pocket,
for all along the ditch
gleams the yellow coin
of trefoil, tormentil, ragwort.

3. Not

This is what doesn't happen:
near midnight, and the Sun
resplendent, having passed
unsetting through the west,
proceeds across the north,
unmaking, in his path,
dark and direction, all
we thought we learned at school.

The Sound of a Diamond Planet

I seem to be surrounded
by things not quite there,

like the fieldmice munching
unseen inside my walls,

the spit of sand
uncovered at low tide,

the slick rock waiting to be
a waterfall again.

A planet, they say,
made all of diamond

resonates in its orbit,
light years beyond

human hearing, its bright sound
broadcast in space.

Wasting Time

Watching wind and tide build a wall,
then smash it, blue into white, water
into air that prickles, glints, mists,
falls to ocean again. Watching water lunge
at land, take a bite, suck itself back,
watching this happen over and over
because it is never the same twice,
nothing the sea does is ever
exactly repeated or predictable.
Today the foam is white, driving in
with a south wind behind it, covering
the whole bay with bleached-bone lace;
yesterday rain swelled the burn,
brought the peat down in veins that seeped
gold and brown through the sea, edged it
with a lion's mane. *I wasted time*
said the king, but who is to say?
Waste time, spend it, use it, the one thing
you cannot do is keep it. Everything is
once: the waves that caught the light
while you worked, travelled, had children,
are gone now, and you missed them
a million times, as you missed
and will miss most of the world.
You let the scent of honeysuckle,
stealing from the wall, beguile you,
but behind it somewhere the salt
of wrack passes you by, and when you hear
a loved voice or the rarest music,
always, on the edge of polite
attention, you are listening out
for the sea.

The Eye

Across the bay, they're building a house
with a glass wall, panes all the way up

into the gable, windows that wrap
around corners for a view as wide

as sea and sky, to take in Sumburgh Head,
Auriga, every passing vessel

and pod of orca, storm-force gales,
anvil clouds, the cliffs of Levenwick,

the waxing moon lighting a track
clear to Fair Isle. This huge eye,

lidless, unfillable, as hungry
for every last object it can rest on

as if it were mortal, knowing how soon
light goes by; how little time it has.

The USDAW Mural, Cardiff

1.

If you walked through the wide, six-arched window
on Minsky's wall, you would leave behind the street

out back of the mall, between the fruit market
and the cathedral; you would find yourself

on the lower slopes of a steep cliff,
gazing up to where it scrapes cloud,

or down on an empty ocean. And you *could*
step through; where glass should be, gulls hover

each side of the frame, and a small climber
with ropes and a hard-hat is just scrambling

over the sill towards us, abandoning
salt in the air, his dream of ascent,

so it seems, for a gum-crusted pavement
anchoring his boots to the here and now.

2.

It was never meant to be like this.
On our side of that window, plain to see,

we stand in a fine hall, some library
or debating chamber, a room for thought

and argument, built to such a height,
no-one could look around and think small,

not when the gulls fly through at eye level
saying *there is no glass between you*

and the light. For if we can follow
them, our climber too can choose to come

up in the world, into this high room
where, above the window, carved in stone

and massive pride, run the words UNION
OF SHOP DISTRIBUTIVE AND ALLIED WORKERS.

3.

How came we to fall so far below
that room's measure, as to see nothing

but the painted side of a shabby building,
a fake, a backdrop for bin-bags?

The marble sill bears graffiti tags:
sea and sky have dulled to the same blue.

That ocean leapt, when the colours were new,
wings gleamed; you felt the chill in the high room.

Now, if you want to, you can see the sham:
paint flaking, a patch naked altogether,

neither cloud nor cliff, but peeling plaster.
You need not see the gulls using glass

like air, the lofty space that draws the eyes
upward, the words, the world through the window.

Cardiff: January

The fountain froze
into a grey, scuffed bezel

for dead bus tickets
and a bronze boy.

He'd posed for years, nude
in the municipal pond,

a little battered, discoloured
by casual vandals,

but just for a while, sheathed
shoulder to heel in ice, chilled

but stylish, like the girls
who go clubbing coatless

on January nights, he gleamed
green through the glassy suiting

that fitted him so well.
Winter sun lit rainbows

all down the long stalactite
dangling from his fingers

like an ivory cane
he might be about to twirl.

Ghosts of Cardiff

It isn't so much leaving the place now:
anyone can do that, walk away
from the place that is now. It is having to leave
all the thens, the places it has been
in its time. To move through the avenue
of chestnuts in Pontcanna Fields, knowing
their wide leaves slanted light just that way
on Buffalo Bill's whooping Indian riders.

Most streets are more crowded than they look:
down by Victoria Park, it's easy to miss
the seal that used to haul itself, now and then,
out of its pond and go for a short waddle
in the side roads, being greeted by neighbours.
Billy all his life, till he died
and became female: statue now, maybe,
but still a damp slap-slap on the pavement.

And if you walk down Clare Street, every tidy front
the same now, you might not notice the ghost-house
covered in grievances, black words on white board,
looking like a mind turned inside out.
As for the bronze boy, butterfly on wrist,
from Thompson's Park, he goes walkabout
with metal thieves so often, it's anyone's guess
what street you might find him strolling on.

But in St Mary Street, look out for martyrs:
Rawlins White roams, bemused, the racks
of expensive suiting in Howell's menswear,
his fisherman's boots sinking into the carpet
as he seeks the fire that consumed him.
Poor Dic Penderyn is nothing but a voice,
raw, shocked, echoing round the market roof
from his scaffold: *Oh Lord, here is iniquity.*

Down the Bay, the *Terra Nova* is conned
out of harbour; tramp-steamers leach coal
and iron to the wide world, bring back languages,
and all along Westgate, the Golate, the Hayes,
you can hear Charlie's high-pitched cackle,
the soft pads of his little wrapped dogs
and, in December, the raucous handbell,
the cracked carols, under a Santa hat.

They are so many, you have to thread a path
along pavements; they clump in conversational knots
at street corners. They hang out in the Taff Vale
and the Panorama, they are on their way to meetings
at the Cory Hall and the Engineers' Institute.
They know this city backwards, and however
ghosts are meant to smell, the heavy sweetness
of brewing malt hangs everywhere they go.

Capybara Moments

When, on a winter morning, out
early, before the binmen come round,

you see down the street, some way off,
huddled on the pavement by the gate

of some terraced house, a small group
of capybara, two adults and a baby,

the important thing is to stop. Not to go
a step closer. Take time first

to sense them, their wariness, the barest
twitch of a snout, the tension in their crouch,

the way pale sunlight brindles their fur
until it almost glitters. Wait

while they narrate themselves: how
came they here, so far from the Amazon,

escaped or abandoned, what do their feet
make of city streets, what happens next?

Then, when you do at last go closer,
when with your every step they become

other, resolving themselves slowly
into a pile of black, frosted bin-bags,

the first story will still go on
being true, holding the place

it shaped in your mind, in that moment
when there were capybara.

Later

Passing the park gates, the child
urges his mother through.

She says "later", tries to plod on,
steering the buggy one-handed

while he wails and hauls sideways.
They must go home now

to feed the baby (wide-eyed
and oblivious). It is lunchtime:

they will have something nice.
He doesn't want it;

he wants what is passing,
the park, now, this minute.

He is young; it may be
"later" means nothing yet,

or he doesn't trust it.
There is a duck

strolling on the grass,
its green head glinting;

why should he believe
it will still be there

when they come back with bread?
If they come back.

When they go home,
he knows already,

the duck in the park
may be pushed back

behind meals, hoovering,
phone calls, behind hours

or days, although there is nothing
that matters so much,

right now, as its low chuckle,
the blue flash near its wing.

It's posing among the last
canna lilies, their edges

beginning to brown. My mother
was fond of lilies. The sun

has broken free of cloud,
for how long; the duck's head

dazzles, metallic blues
and purples in the green,

and I think the child is right
to scream as he diminishes

down the street, believing
there is no later.

Catching Up

My mother becomes younger by the day
since she died; she has only ten years

on me now. Side by side, we'd be sisters:
she, still, the bossy elder who knows best

about everything, but that won't last.
I shall look back at her from my seventies

before long, saying *this is how it is,
the age you never reached.* Maybe

it will be she, then, who follows me,
and I who show her places I know

that are new to her. More likely, though,
I shall address my wisdom to her back

as she grows smaller, retracing the track
I came by, still going her own way.

Different Corridors

A moment ago, while you still slept,
they were all in the same story:
the ship, your mother, that job you left.
Now, as the room comes back, they are beginning
to unravel: you catch at a fact, a face,
but they slip by, each diminishing down
a different corridor, calling round corners
like children playing chase in some old house.

And your mind cannot help but go
to the author who is losing the plot,
who stood on the rostrum staring down
at the page where his words had come loose
from their meanings, had freed themselves so far
as to become not even patterns but penstrokes;
he liked the curly ones best, but how to turn them
back into ideas was beyond him.

It is an old house; some rooms we have not seen
in years, and the time is coming
when the way home, old friends, names of things
we have always known, our own children,
will be off down different corridors,
laughing round corners while we stand puzzled.
How random are these dreams, that seemed to fit
so well together, while we were sleeping.

Skeleton

30 Years War, Landenberg

Jaw set
agape, head thrown back,

empty eye-sockets watching
death come down.

No soldier,
hardened to this,

but a young woman
in a taken town,

murdered, discarded
in a ditch-grave

with all the others
spoiled in the war.

In her display case
she gives off,

like a foul smell,
the sudden knowledge

that nothing
will serve; she is looking

into eyes untroubled
by daughters

or sisters, this girl
whose scream unmakes

glass and distance, who died
screaming.

The Vanishing Bishop

Dig a hole in the ground
hereabouts, you'll hit plague pits
like as not, or a Roman god.
I hit a bishop.

My spade sliced into a fibrous mass,
then slid under. I lifted, thinking
roots, but rotten coffin-wood
came away. Left his face

staring up, for all the world
as if I'd disturbed him dozing.
Red stubble on his rosy cheeks:
could have died yesterday,

but for the full-bottomed wig
that no-one's worn in centuries.
I shouted: sent someone off
to the museum,

and stayed with him. And I swear
it was no time, just him and me
together, content not to speak,
like two old neighbours.

But before anyone came,
that face, full lips, firm lines,
furrowed brow, did something
I'd only ever seen

in a fire, when a big log
has burned so long, it's ash
in the shape of wood, nothing
holding it together

but habit. His whole face
suddenly settled, fell in on itself,
letting go its last memory
of who he'd been.

When the scientists came pointing
cameras at all angles
of their black-wigged skeleton,
I wanted to say

you only just missed him; he was here
with me a moment ago,
a worried man; he had a pout
and a red beard starting.

The Sailor Who Fell from the Rigging

He's a bone-hoard, laid
golden on the table,
piecemeal, dislocated

in the naval hospital
at Haslar, this casualty
from Nelson's day. Skull

a cup, eye-sockets empty
bezels for aquamarine
or jet. The carved vertebrae,

links in a polished chain
that has come unstrung
since, long ago, a man

fell, his limbs flailing,
in that last instant
when limbs would do his bidding,

before every joint
of arms and legs splintered
on the deck; made a patient

of a seaman. His scarred
bones were knitting together,
twisted, no doubt, awkward,

when the usual fever
sank him in the dark.
He is turned to treasure:

the ribs' symmetrical fretwork,
the pendant branches
of phalanges, the serpentine torc

two clavicles make. Riches
beyond price, broken past
restoring, such choice pieces
as cannot be replaced.

Footnote

Per Heaman, Swedish sailor, turned pirate
for the *Jane's* silver freight. He helped heave
the captain overboard, bludgeoned the mate
but left a weeping cabin-boy alive

to bear witness against him. At his trial
he lied, forswore himself, confessed nothing,
and in the death-cart, among the catcalls,
he stood up in his chains, waving and bowing.

Offered a last request, he paused, replied:
"Don't tell my mother how I lived and died."

A Good Sunrise

Travelling early, you form the hope
of a good sunrise, like all the dawns

you've slept through, waking to remnant ribbons
of another missed spectacular.

Face pressed to the train window, you stare
beyond glass, to the dark passing,

and wait for the turn, for clusters and strings
of light to become roads and villages,

for colour to lap at the edges
of sky, then bleed, run, flood

as far as eyes reach. It'd be good,
but what happens, more often than not,

is as simple as slow-growing light.
The dark just ends, the world just takes shape.

The Talents

Why would those born with wings
ever shed them? Here's an ant-swarm
on its only flight, learning

to lean back in the arm
of air, letting it borrow
them, riding the thermals,

and then they come down, go
to ground. After one escape,
after tasting sky, they burrow

into earth, leaving scraps
of discarded freedom, transparent
and brittle, tracing-paper

wings littering pavements,
stiffening, sun-dried.
In the memory of ants,

no rush, no glide,
no coupling in air;
they live satisfied

with tracks worn familiar,
with work-routines
embedded in their nature.

The swollen machine
that mated on the wing
breeds trapped, unseen,

where the blind things
slither, smelling dark,
hearing grains fall, never missing

the eyes that should sparkle
from their soft, healed bezels.
You'd think they lacked
nothing at all.

The Door Open

Say you go away
on business: you are some time
from home, and when you come back,

a man has moved in.
His eyes hold yours, his tones
persuade, his words command

your wife's rapt attention.
Behind their hands
neighbours grin. They are mistaken.

She is a good woman;
he is a good man. He believes
in a new way, afire,

and she has caught light
by him. Your house is full
of bright-faced strangers

planning a new world.
You liked the old one,
but she is alive

as you have never seen her.
You sense the centre
shifting, feel yourself spinning

out to the edge. Your children
call him father. There is love
enough for everyone.

Perhaps you are not surprised
to hear yourself offer
your house for his meetings,

but in your study,
keeping apart, listening
to the eager friends

building paradise on earth
across the passage,
you are never sure

if it is care
for her good repute
or some other thing,

harder to name,
that makes you always leave
the door open.

Naglfar

They'll be coming to end the world some day,
sicking wolves on to swallow the sun and moon,
stamping crops flat. Their faces slabs of stone,
their eyes tiny. Nothing you can say
will make odds to them; they will not stay
their hand for kindness or reason.
Their fingers snuff stars, not even for fun
but indifferently, along their way.

And they will come on the ship Naglfar,
made all of dead men's nails, that cannot sail
until the world has enough of us,
the kind and the cruel both, until the fill
of all those graves takes the shape of our killer,
our leavings at last cobbled into use.

Strauss

The ostrich's petals are shaggy,
chrysanthemum-bronze and cream
above their oasis cushion.
The neck is a feathery stem

of maidenhair fern, and it flexes
and dips with a dancer's pace
like a girl being whirled round a ballroom,
some frothy young Viennese miss

who will prove less flighty than flightless,
confined to a vase, to the ground,
to a body, a life that keeps moving
around and around and around.

Letter to Dr Johnson

Dear Dr Johnson, I am writing this note,
if you'll excuse a stranger's approach,

beside the statue of your cat Hodge,
whose eyes are fixed on your old front door

as if you might come out with an oyster
or two. That odd thought of yours

won't leave me: *we shall receive no letters
in the grave*, however companionable

we be, however desperate for people
and their news, their voices. I shall seal this

and slip it under your door, just in case
on the other side, disembodied but portly,

a dishevelled ghost is waiting daily
for a letter to land on the mat.

How To Leave

Bit by bit. Start at the top
of the Street; work your way along

the little shops, looking, stopping
one last time, as if there were somewhere

you might have missed. At the far end,
where you have to turn down to the harbour,

thinking *was there anything else*, conscious
of turning your back, you feel the first

lurch of loss. But the port is alive
with small boats, trawlers, supply ships;

from the North Ness you can see back over
the whole curve, just before you round

the headland and put it behind you. It gets
no easier; you pause at the museum

to pass some time. An hour goes by
before you know. People have written songs

about leaving this harbour, slow airs
mostly. When you set your face

north again, you are walking toward
the Co-Op, and you can tell yourself

you are just out shopping, picking up
a few provisions, but then

you pass the door without going in,
and now what you can see before you

is the ferry terminal. The white ship
squats, its lines unlovely. You board it anyway.

What makes this possible is knowing
you sail out southwards, that the town

has not quite left yet, will be back
briefly, bit by bit, as you go by

leaning on the rail: the museum, the Ness,
the grey town hunched on the hill,

just not for long. Now the harbour
comes in sight; now it is falling

aft; now you round the Knab
and it is gone. However many times

you practise this, it always ends
looking back down a long wake.

Return

13th October 2010

What the earth takes, it gives again: look,
do not fathers, brothers, sons rise

from the ground, their eyes shaded, in case
they hanker for the dark? Do not

marriages restart from this minute,
like a stopped clock set going again,

are not hasty words, that might have been
last words, now air? Each tenant, his leasehold

on light renewed, is given back the world,
we too: how not, even though we know

few are paroled, none pardoned. Just now
they stand for all who were not granted leave

and will not be, as if indeed love
could go down deep enough to bring us back.

Acknowledgements

Some of these poems have previously appeared in *Agenda,* *Eyewear, Horizon Review, Island Review, Literature and Belief,* *Magma, New Walk, New Writing Scotland 30,* The *Peterloo* competition anthology, *PN Review, Poetry Review, Poetry Scotland, Poetry* *Wales, Roundyhouse, The New Shetlander, These Islands, We Sing* (edited by Kevin MacNeil, Polygon), the Vital Synz Edwin Morgan poetry competition website and the *Warwick Review.*